Dominoes

Sherlock Holmes
The Blue Diamond

OXFORD

OXFORD

UNIVERSITY PRESS

Great Clarendon Street, Oxford OX2 6DP

Oxford University Press is a department of the University of Oxford.
It furthers the University's objective of excellence in research, scholarship,
and education by publishing worldwide in

Oxford New York

Auckland Cape Town Dar es Salaam Hong Kong Karachi
Kuala Lumpur Madrid Melbourne Mexico City Nairobi
New Delhi Shanghai Taipei Toronto

With offices in

Argentina Austria Brazil Chile Czech Republic France Greece
Guatemala Hungary Italy Japan Poland Portugal Singapore
South Korea Switzerland Thailand Turkey Ukraine Vietnam

OXFORD and OXFORD ENGLISH are registered trade marks of
Oxford University Press in the UK and in certain other countries

ISBN-13: 978 0 19 424340 7
ISBN-10: 0 19 424340 0

A complete recording of this Dominoes edition of *The Blue Diamond*
is available on cassette ISBN 0 19 424356 7

Printed in China

ACKNOWLEDGEMENTS

The publisher would like to thank the following for permission to reproduce images: Corbis pp 42
(Mona Lisa/Gianni dagli Orti), 43 (Goering/Bettmann); The Ronald Grant Archive p 40
(Jessica Fletcher), (Hercule Poirot); Hulton Getty Images pp 12, 42 (Mona Lisa
recovered/Topical Press Agency); The Kobal Collection p 40 (Fox Mulder and Dana
Scully); Netherlands Institute for Cultural Heritage p 43 (Hans van Meegeren, Christ and
the Adulteress, 1941/Photo Tim Koster, ICN, Rijswijk, Amsterdam); Photofest NY p 40
(Inspector Gadget/© DIC Animation/Warner)

Dominoes

SERIES EDITORS: BILL BOWLER AND SUE PARMINTER

Sherlock Holmes

The Blue Diamond

SIR ARTHUR CONAN DOYLE

Text adaptation by Bill Bowler

Illustrated by Susan Scott

LEVEL ONE ■ 400 HEADWORDS

Sir Arthur Conan Doyle (1859–1930), born in Edinburgh, Scotland, is best known as the creator of Sherlock Holmes. He started writing after working as a doctor and soon became one of the world's best-known authors. His adventure story *The Lost World* is also available in Dominoes.

OXFORD

BEFORE READING

1 **Here are some of the people in *The Blue Diamond*.**
What work do they do? Use a dictionary to help you.

Name: Mr Peterson
Work: ....

Name: Mr Baker
Work: ....

Name: James Ryder
Work: ....

Name: John Horner
Work: ....

Name: Catherine Cusack
Work: ....

Name: Mrs Hudson
Work: ....

Name: Mr Windigate
Work: ....

Name: Mr Breckinridge
Work: ....

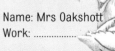

Name: Mrs Oakshott
Work: ....

2 **Which of these people help to steal the diamond?**

Sherlock Holmes
The Blue Diamond

CHAPTER 1 *An old hat*

M y name's Dr Watson, and I'm a good friend of the famous detective Sherlock Holmes. Two days after Christmas last year I went to his house – 221B Baker Street. I wanted to say 'Happy Christmas!' to him. When I arrived, I found him in the **sitting-room**. He was by the window with some **newspapers** next to him. There was an old hat on a chair near him, and he had a **magnifying glass** in his hand.

'You're working on something,' I said. 'Shall I go?'

'No,' said Holmes. 'Sit down and look at that interesting old hat over there.'

Holmes /hǝʊmz/

diamond a very expensive stone that usually has no colour

sitting-room the room in a house where people sit and talk

newspaper people read about things that happen every day in this

magnifying glass when you look through this, small things are big

I sat down. It was cold out in the street, but it was nice and warm in Holmes's sitting room.

'Why are you interested in that old hat? Is it something to do with a **crime**?' I asked.

Holmes laughed. 'Not a crime, no,' he said. 'I got it from Peterson, the **doorman** at the Baker Street Hotel.

'He found it in the street and brought it here on Christmas Day for me to look at. He also brought a dead **bird** with him – a good fat Christmas **goose** – at the same time.

'I gave the goose back to him this morning. He's **cooking** it at his house now and he's going to eat it for dinner tonight.'

'First it was a hat, and now you're talking about a goose!' I said. 'I don't understand.'

'Then let's begin when it all began,' said Holmes.

'At about four o'clock in the morning of Christmas Day, Peterson went home after work. When he got to Tottenham Court Road he saw, in the street in front of him, a tall man with a goose over his **shoulder**. Peterson walked behind him for some time.

'There were some young men in the street in front of them. Suddenly one of them hit the tall man's hat off his head and it **fell** into the road. Then the tall man **tried** to hit the young man with his **walking stick**, but by accident he broke the window of a shop behind him.

'At that moment Peterson ran to the man to help him, but the tall man ran away. Perhaps he felt bad about breaking the shop window. Perhaps he thought that Peterson – in his doorman's coat and hat – was a policeman.

crime killing someone, or taking money from someone

doorman a man working at a hotel; he opens the front door for visitors

bird an animal that can fly; you can eat some birds

goose (*plural* **geese**) a large, usually white bird; people sometimes eat it at Christmas

cook to make things for people to eat

shoulder this is between your arm and your neck

fall (*past* **fell**) to go down suddenly

try to want to do something but not to do it well

walking stick a long, thin piece of wood; you use this to help you to walk

'When he ran, he left his
Christmas bird in the street next to his
hat. The young men ran away at the same
time, so Peterson took the goose and the hat home
with him, and the next day he brought them here.

'There was an interesting little ticket on the goose's left
leg,' said Holmes. 'It said "For Mr and Mrs Henry Baker".
We can find the letters H.B. in the hat too.'

'Oh . . . the **owner** of the hat and the goose
is called Henry Baker,' I said.

'Yes,' answered Holmes. 'But my dear Watson this
doesn't help us very much. There are hundreds of
Henry Bakers in London. I gave the goose back to
Peterson this morning,' he went on, 'and I said to him:
"Have this for your dinner!" I didn't want it to go bad,
you know.'

owner the person
that something
belongs to

'Did Mr Baker put an **advertisement** in the newspaper about his hat and goose?' I asked.

'No,' answered Holmes.

'Then how can we find him?'

'Well, perhaps his hat can help us,' said Holmes. 'Here's my magnifying glass, Watson. Now, you be a detective for a minute or two. What can you tell me about the owner of this hat?'

I took the magnifying glass and looked at the hat. It was black but old, and very, very dirty. I saw the letters H.B. in it. For me it was no different from any other old black hat.

'I can see nothing,' I said, and I gave the hat back to my friend.

'Excuse me, Watson. You *do* see, but you don't think about what you see.'

'All right!' I said. 'What can *you* see in this hat?'

'The owner of this hat is an **intelligent** man,' said Holmes. 'He was once rich and is now **poor**. His wife loved him once but she doesn't love him now. And he's thirty or forty years old.

'Well, perhaps I'm slow, Holmes, but I don't understand,' I said. 'Why is he an intelligent man, do you think?'

Holmes put the hat on his head. It came down to his **nose**. 'This is a big hat. A man with a big hat has a big head, and a man with a big head has a big **brain**. A man with a big brain thinks a lot.'

'But you say he was once rich and is now poor. Why?'

'The hat is three years old. I remember these hats were in all the shops then. They were very expensive too.

'Three years ago this man **bought** a good hat, so he was rich then. But he has no money to buy a new hat

advertisement you pay to put this in a newspaper

intelligent quick-thinking

poor not rich

nose this is between your eyes

brain this is in your head and you think with it

buy (*past* **bought**) to give money for something

now, so these days he is poor.'

'All right,' I said. 'But you say he is in his thirties or forties. How does the hat tell you this?'

'Well, when I looked carefully at the hat with my magnifying glass, I could see some **grey** hairs in it. People usually get grey hair in their thirties or forties.'

'I see. But what about his wife? You say she doesn't love him.'

'Because the hat is very dirty. When a woman loves her husband, she cleans his hat for him.'

'Perhaps he hasn't got a wife.'

'Yes, he has. Remember the ticket on the goose's leg.'

'Ah yes,' I said. 'You have an answer for everything.'

At that moment the door opened and Peterson the hotel doorman ran into the room. He looked very excited.

'The goose, Mr Holmes. The goose!' he said.

'What's the matter with the goose?' asked Holmes. 'Did it come back from the dead and fly off through the **kitchen** window?'

'No, Mr Holmes. My wife found this in the bird!' Peterson opened his hand. There was a beautiful blue diamond in it.

grey the colour between white and black

kitchen the room in a house where people cook

READING CHECK

Are these sentences true or false?

		True	False
a	The story happens in December.	☑	☐
b	Holmes tells his friend Watson about a tall man with an old hat.	☐	☐
c	The tall man left a yellow bird in the street.	☐	☐
d	A hotel doorman – Peterson – gave the hat and the bird to Holmes.	☐	☐
e	Holmes gave the bird to Watson.	☐	☐
f	Peterson's wife found a green diamond in the bird.	☐	☐

WORD WORK

a magnifying glass

1 **Look at the pictures and complete the crossword.**

2 **Read the blue squares and write the name of another blue jewel.** S _ _ _ _ _ _ _

3 Find the words from Chapter 1 and write the sentences.

a She's *cooking* it in the *kitchen* now.

She's cooking it in the kitchen now.

b ADVERTISEMENT – Do you want to *buy* a new *hat* ?

....

c He's an *intelligent* man, with a red *nose* and *grey* hair.

....

d The *crime* didn't happen in the *sitting room* .

....

e He *tried* to catch it before it *fell* .

....

f The *doorman* isn't the owner of the *hat* .

....

g The story of the blue *diamond* is very interesting.

....

GUESS WHAT

What happens in the next chapter?
Write *Holmes*, *Watson*, *Peterson* or *Nobody* in each sentence.

a .... calls the police.

b .... knows about the owner of the diamond.

c .... takes Peterson to the police.

d .... keeps the diamond.

e .... writes to the Countess.

f .... puts an advertisement in the newspaper.

CHAPTER 2 *The Blue Diamond*

countess the wife of a rich, important man

disappear to go away suddenly

jewel an expensive stone

pay (*past* **paid**) to give money for something

When Sherlock Holmes saw the diamond in the doorman's hand he sat up. 'Well, well, Peterson,' he said. ' What a wonderful thing to find in a goose. Do you know what you have in your hand?'

'I think it's a diamond, Mr Holmes. Is it expensive?'

'Yes, it is,' said Holmes. 'This is the **Countess** of Morcar's blue diamond. It **disappeared** a week ago.'

'How do you know that?' I said.

'Watson, you must read the newspapers more often. There's an advertisement in *The Times* today about it. Here, look.'

Holmes gave the advertisement to me.

Then Holmes spoke to the doorman. 'It's a very expensive **jewel**, Peterson. The Countess **paid** about £20,000 for it. Last week someone took it from her rooms in the Cosmopolitan Hotel. Now the Countess wants to get her diamond back. She says that she's going to give a thousand pounds to the finder.'

FRIDAY, 27th December 1886 ❧THE TIMES

ADVERTISEMENT

DIAMOND STOLEN!

FIND THE COUNTESS of MORCAR'S DIAMOND AND GET £1,000

'A thousand pounds!' cried Peterson excitedly. Then, without saying more, he sat down in the chair between us. First he looked at Holmes and then he looked at me.

'The diamond disappeared five days ago, I think,' I said.

'Yes,' answered Holmes. 'They say a young man, John Horner, took it. Here's a newspaper **report** about the case.'

Holmes gave an old newspaper to me and I read the report.

A DIAMOND DISAPPEARS FROM THE COSMOPOLITAN HOTEL

The Countess of Morcar's blue diamond disappeared from her room at the Cosmopolitan Hotel on the 22nd of this month. The police think John Horner, 26 years old, took the diamond from a jewel box when he went to **repair** the window in the room.

James Ryder, the **assistant manager** of the hotel, told the **court**: 'I took Horner to the Countess's room but then I went away for some time. When I came back, Horner wasn't there, and I found the open box, without the jewel in it, on the table next to the bed.'

Catherine **Cusack**, the countess's **maid**, spoke next: 'I heard Mr Ryder call and I ran to the Countess's room. There I found Ryder with the jewel box in front of him.'

The police found Horner at his home later that day, but they couldn't find the diamond.

Later, Detective Bradstreet spoke to the court: 'When I said "You're a diamond **thief**!" Horner hit me.'

Soon after that Horner told the court angrily: 'You've got the wrong man. I didn't take the Countess's diamond. I'm not a thief.'

Bradstreet then told the court: 'Horner went to **prison** once before for being a thief. I say he took the diamond.'

The **case** goes to the **High Court** next week.

---

report some writing in a newspaper

repair to make something that is broken work again

assistant manager an important job in a hotel

court the police take someone here when they think he or she did something wrong

Cusack /ˈkjuːsæk/

maid a woman who works in a rich person's house, or in a hotel

thief a person who takes things without asking

prison a place where people must stay when they do something wrong

case when the police work to find answers

High Court the most important court in the country

'Well, that's the newspaper report about the diamond,' said Holmes. 'Now we need to understand how the jewel left the Countess of Morcar's room in the Cosmopolitan hotel and arrived in Tottenham Court Road in a goose.

'You see, Watson, there *is* a crime in this case. Here's the diamond. The diamond came from the goose, and the goose came from Mr Henry Baker – the man with the old hat.

'I know you felt a little bored when I told you all about Mr Baker, but now we must find him. Where and how does he come into the case of the blue diamond? The answer to these two questions is most important.'

'But how can we find him?' I asked.

'Through a newspaper advertisement,' answered Holmes.

He took a pen and began to write.

Did you lose a goose and a black hat some days ago in Tottenham Court Road?

Are you called Henry Baker?

Please come to 221B Baker Street this evening at 6.30 to get your things.

'There. That says it all, I think,' said Holmes.

'Yes, but is he going to read it?' I asked.

'Yes, Watson, I think he is. He's a poor man, remember. At the time he was afraid because of his accident with the shop window, but now I **believe** he feels very sorry about running away and thinks: "Why did I leave that bird in the street?"

'Perhaps he looked for a newspaper advertisement about it yesterday. I think he's going to look again today, too.

'What's more, we've got his name in the advertisement, so I believe his friends are going to see it and tell him about it.'

'Yes, I see,' I said.

Holmes gave some money to the doorman and said: 'Peterson, please go down to the newspaper offices and put this advertisement in all the evening newspapers.'

'Very good, **sir**. And shall I leave the diamond with you, sir?'

'Yes, Peterson. And, I say, Peterson, after you leave the newspaper offices, can you buy a goose and bring it back here? We need a new bird for Mr Henry Baker when he comes. Your family is eating the old one for dinner today, so he can't have that.'

The doorman went out of the door and down the street.

believe to think that something is true

sir you say this when you talk to a rich or important man

11

READING CHECK

Correct the mistakes in these sentences.

a The Countess paid £2,000 for the diamond. *20,000*

b It disappeared from the Countess's house.

c The police think James Ryder took it.

d Holmes understands how the diamond got into the goose.

e Holmes wants to find John Horner.

f Peterson leaves the diamond with his wife.

g Peterson must buy a hat for Henry Baker.

WORD WORK

1 Correct the underlined words in these sentences.

a Their <u>paid</u>, Catherine, is only sixteen. ......*maid*......

b The <u>jowel</u> is very expensive. ....

c You are Sherlock Holmes, I <u>relieve</u>. ....

d When did the diamond <u>disapprove</u>, <u>sit</u>? ....

e You took that without asking. You're a <u>chief</u>. ....

2 Use the letters in brackets to complete the last words in these sentences. Write the words in the crossword.

a I work at the hotel. I'm the ssstnt mngr. (aaaaei)

b Detective Bradstreet saw Horner in crt. (ou)

c I brought this here for you to rpr. (aei)

d You are a very bad man and you must go to prsn. (io)

e Would you like to be a Cntss? (eou)

f This case is very important. It must go to the Hgh Crt. (iou)

g Have you read the newspaper rprt? (eo)

| a | a | s | s | i | s | t | a | n | t | m | a | n | a | g | e | r |

3 Read the blue squares and write the name of the country where the Countess's jewel box came from.

M _ _ _ _ _ _

GUESS WHAT

What happens in the next chapter?
Tick the boxes.   Yes   No

a Mr Baker comes to see Holmes.   ☐   ☐

b Baker knows about the diamond in the goose.   ☐   ☐

c Holmes gives Mr Baker the new goose and his old hat. ☐   ☐

d Holmes takes Mr Baker to the police.   ☐   ☐

e Holmes gives Mr Baker the diamond.   ☐   ☐

CHAPTER 3 *Mr Henry Baker*

Holmes took the blue diamond in his hand and looked at it. 'What a beautiful thing!' he said. 'Look at the wonderful colours in it – dark blues and cold whites. All big jewels make people into thieves and killers in the end. This one comes from the south of China, near the **Amoy** river. It's only twenty years old, so it's a young thing, but **already** many **terrible** crimes are happening because of it.

'I'm going to put it in my **safe** now, and then let's write a letter to the Countess of Morcar and say we have her beautiful blue diamond here with us.'

'But Holmes,' I said, 'I don't understand. Is that young man Horner **innocent** after all?'

'I don't know.'

'And what about Henry Baker – the tall man with the hat and the goose? Is he the jewel thief perhaps?'

'No, I don't think he is. I believe he's an innocent man. I don't think he knew there was an expensive diamond in his goose – a jewel worth more than £20,000. But let's wait and see. Perhaps Mr Baker's going to answer our advertisement this evening and then we can learn something more about him.'

'All right,' I said. 'I can come back after work this evening. I'm very interested in the answer to this case.'

'Good,' replied Holmes. 'Dinner is at 7 o'clock.'

I got to Baker Street at 6.30 that evening. There was a tall man already at Sherlock Holmes's front door when I came down the street. He wore a long winter coat and had a Scottish hat on his head. When I arrived next to him the door opened. Mrs Hudson, Holmes's

Amoy /əˈmɔɪ/

already happening earlier than you think

terrible very bad

safe a box that people put expensive things in so thieves can't get them

innocent doing nothing wrong

housekeeper, said 'Good evening' to the two of us, and we went in and upstairs to Holmes's room.

'Mr Henry Baker, I believe!' said Holmes to the man when he came in. 'Please sit down.'

Holmes looked at me and smiled.

'Ah, Watson, good. You are here when we need you.'

Then he looked back at his other visitor.

'Is that your hat, Mr Baker?'

Mr Baker looked at the hat on the chair.

'Yes, sir. That's my hat. There's no question about it.'

housekeeper a woman who looks after a rich person's house

He was a big man with a big head, an intelligent face, and grey hair. I remembered Holmes's words about him.

He wore a dirty old black coat with no shirt under it, but he spoke slowly, quietly and carefully. I looked at him and listened to him and I thought: 'Yes, this is an intelligent man. He was rich once but now he has no money and things aren't easy for him.'

'We found your hat and your goose some days ago,' said Holmes, 'But we couldn't find *you* very easily, Mr Baker. We didn't know your **address**. Why didn't you put an advertisement in the newspaper with your address in it? We waited and waited for an advertisement from you, but saw nothing.'

Mr Baker smiled 'I'm sorry. Advertisements are expensive and I haven't got a lot of money these days. I had once, but not now,' he went on. 'And, well, I thought those young men in Tottenham Court Road had my hat and my goose, and I didn't want to put an expensive advertisement in the newspaper for nothing.'

'I understand,' said Holmes, 'Now, before we say more, I must tell you something about your goose, Mr Baker. I'm sorry but . . . well . . . we ate it yesterday, you know.'

'You ate it!' said our visitor, and he stood up excitedly.

'Yes, well, we didn't want it to go bad, you see. But we bought a nice new goose this morning for you. It's on the table there by the door. Is that all right for you?'

'Oh, yes, yes!' said Mr Baker happily. He sat down again.

'And, let's see, I think we have your old goose's feet, head and everything from inside it in the kitchen. Do

address the number and the street where somebody lives

you want those?'

The man laughed. 'No, no,' he said. 'But I'd like to take that nice new goose home with me, thank you very much.'

Sherlock Holmes looked at me with a little smile. 'Very well,' he said to Mr Baker. 'There is your hat and there is your bird. Please take them. Oh, and, before you go, can you tell me something? Where did you get your goose? I know a lot about geese and that was a very good bird, I can tell you.'

'Well, sir,' said Baker. He stood up and took his hat and the goose in his hands. 'I got that bird at The Alpha, a **pub** near the British **Museum**. This yèar the owner of the pub, Mr Windigate, began a goose club. Every week we all put five or six pence into a money box and at Christmas time we all had the money for a goose.'

With that he said goodbye, and left.

'Well,' said my detective friend. 'That answers one question. Mr Baker is not our diamond thief. Are you hungry, Watson?'

'No, not very.'

'Let's eat later then. We must go to The Alpha at once. We need to speak to Mr Windigate tonight.'

pub a building where people go to have a drink

museum a building where people look at old or interesting things

READING CHECK

Choose the right words to finish the sentences.

a Holmes thinks the diamond is . . .
1 wonderful and good. ☐
2 beautiful but bad. ☑
3 nice and cheap. ☐

b Mr Baker didn't put an advertisement in the newspaper because . . .
1 he wasn't interested in his hat and goose. ☐
2 he thought that the police had his hat and goose. ☐
3 an advertisement is expensive and he doesn't have much money. ☐

c Mr Baker . . .
1 wants his old hat and his old goose. ☐
2 is happy with a new hat and his old goose. ☐
3 is happy with his old hat and the new goose. ☐

d After Mr Baker leaves, Holmes and Watson go to speak to . . .
1 Jack Horner. ☐
2 the young men in Tottenham Court Road. ☐
3 Mr Windigate, the owner of the Alpha. ☐

WORD WORK

Find eight words from the story. Then complete the sentences on page 19.

innocent housekeeper address already pub terrible museum

18

a 'This is a very bad crime.' 'Yes. It's _terrible_ .'

b Holmes put the diamond in his ....

c Holmes's .... is 221B Baker Street.

d Mr Baker is .... He didn't take the diamond.

e Mr Baker was .... at the door when Watson arrived.

f Mrs Hudson is Sherlock Holmes's ....

g The British .... has many old things in it.

h They want to have a drink in the ....

GUESS WHAT

What happens in the next chapter? Tick one picture.

a Mr Windigate can't help Holmes. ☐

b Mr Windigate is the diamond thief. ☐

c Mr Windigate tells Holmes about the geese. ☐

d Mr Windigate knows the diamond thief. ☐

CHAPTER 4 *To Mr Breckinridge's*

H olmes and I put on our coats and hats and went out into the cold winter street. The sky was dark over our heads. We walked east, and in a quarter of an hour we stood in front of The Alpha. Holmes opened the door and we went in.

In the pub the owner, Mr Windigate, gave us some **beer**.

'Is this beer good?' Holmes asked him. 'I ask because I know your geese are very good. Mr Henry Baker told us all about your goose club.'

'Ah, yes. But those geese weren't our geese. They came from a man with a little shop in Covent Garden. Breckinridge is his name.'

'Thank you, my good man,' said Holmes. We paid for our beer and drank it. Then we walked out of the warm pub and into the cold night again.

'Now for Covent Garden,' said Holmes, and we walked

beer a yellow or brown drink

down the street past the British Museum. 'Remember, Watson, it all began with a goose, but it finishes with seven years in prison for young Mr Horner. Perhaps we can learn more about this interesting case in Mr Breckinridge's shop.'

We walked south and soon came to Mr Breckinridge's shop. Breckinridge and a boy were at the door. It was nearly time to close for the night.

'Good evening. It's a cold night,' said Holmes.

'How can I help you?' asked Breckinridge.

Holmes looked at the empty shop window. 'No geese, I see,' he said.

'There are some in that other shop – there behind you.'

'Ah, but I came to you because I hear your geese are very good. "Breckinridge's birds are the best," he said.'

'Who said that?'

'The owner of The Alpha.'

'Ah, yes. He had twenty-four of my geese two days before Christmas.'

'They were very good birds too. Where did you get them?'

'I'm not going to tell you!' said Breckinridge angrily. 'Again and again people come and talk to me about those geese and I don't like it. I paid good money for them, I took them to The Alpha and then I forgot all about them. And then all the questions began. "Where are the geese?" "How much do you want for them?" "Who did you **sell** them to?" Why are people interested in them? I don't know. They aren't the only geese in London, you know.'

'I know,' said Holmes. 'But who asked you all those questions before? Not me. I had nothing to do with that, you know. But now I need your help. We ate a goose at The Alpha, and I say it was a country goose, but my good friend, Dr Watson here, says it was a London goose. Which of us is right? It's an important question. Five pounds goes to the **winner**.'

'Well then, you lose and your friend is the winner,' said Breckinridge. 'That goose came from London.'

'I can't believe that,' said Holmes.

'A pound says I'm right.'

'Very well,' said Holmes, and he took out a pound. 'I'm ready to pay. But I know you're going to lose your money.'

Breckinridge laughed. 'Bring me the books, Bill,' he said. The boy brought two books to him.

Breckinridge opened the little one. 'This is my address

sell (*past* **sold**) to take money for something

winner the person who gets the right answer

book,' he said. 'When people sell their geese to me their addresses go in here – country people on the left and town people on the right. The numbers after every name are **page** numbers in my big book.'

'Read out the third name on the right,' said Breckinridge.

'Mrs **Oakshott**, 117 Brixton Road. Number 249,' read Holmes.

Then Breckinridge opened the big book. 'And this is my "IN and OUT" book,' he said. 'Let's look at page 249. Here we are. Mrs Oakshott. What can you see for December 22nd?'

'Twenty-four geese from Mrs O,' read Holmes. 'All twenty-four to Mr Windigate at the Alpha.'

'There. What do you say now?' said Breckinridge.

Holmes put his pound into Breckinridge's hand angrily.

page this book has forty-four pages

Oakshott /ˈəʊkʃɒt/

READING CHECK

Put these sentences in the correct order. Number them 1–7.

a   Mr Breckinridge is angry with Holmes. ☐

b   Mr Breckinridge tells Holmes about Mrs Oakshott. ☐

c   Holmes and Watson go to Covent Garden. ☐

d   Holmes and Watson go to the Alpha. ☐

e   Holmes asks Mr Breckinridge about the geese. ☐

f   Holmes gives Mr Breckinridge a pound. ☐

g   Mr Windigate tells Holmes about Mr Breckinridge's shop. ☐

WORD WORK

Complete the sentences with words from the story.

a   'Can I p _a_y you now?'

b   'Yes, of course I want to s _ _ _ this goose.'

c   'Can I have a bottle of b _ _ _ please?'

d   'Look at p _ _ _ 24 in your books.'

e   'You're the w _ _ _ _ _ _'

24

GUESS WHAT

What happens in the next chapter? Tick the pictures.

a Holmes feels . . .

☐ angry with Mr Breckinridge.　☐ happy about the case.　☐ tired.

b Holmes and Watson go to . . .

☐ Mrs Oakshott's.　☐ 221B Baker Street.　☐ The Cosmopolitan Hotel.

c They speak to . . .

☐ Mrs Oakshott.　☐ the Countess's maid.　☐ the hotel's assistant manager.

CHAPTER 5 *A weak little man*

weak not strong

shout to say loudly and angrily

In the street Holmes stopped. Suddenly he wasn't angry; he began to laugh. 'You see, Watson,' he said. 'Breckinridge didn't want to tell me Mrs Oakshott's name and address at first. But later, when he saw he could easily get a pound from me, he told me everything. And he said something very interesting when he got angry. Did you hear? Other people are asking questions about those geese.'

Suddenly there was a lot of noise from Mr Breckinridge's shop behind us. We looked back at it.

Breckinridge stood, tall and angry, in front of his shop door. A **weak** little man stood in front of him in the street.

'Look, you,' Breckinridge **shouted**. 'I don't want to hear any more about those geese. Mrs Oakshott can come and speak to me when she wants, but not you. You have nothing to do with it. Did I get the geese from you?'

'No, but one was *my* goose, I tell you,' cried the little man.

'Then ask Mrs Oakshott for it.'

'But she told me "Ask Mr Breckinridge for it."'

'Well, that's nothing to do with me. I don't want to hear any more from you. Do you understand? Now go away!'

Breckinridge closed his shop door angrily and the little man ran off down the dark street.

'Perhaps we don't need to visit Mrs Oakshott in Brixton Road after all,' said Holmes to me quietly. 'Let's talk to that man. Perhaps he can help us.'

Holmes walked quickly up behind the little man and put a hand on his shoulder. The man stopped and looked back over his shoulder at us. His face was white.

'Who are you? What do you want?' he asked weakly.

job work

'Excuse me,' said Holmes. 'But I heard your questions to that shop owner. I think I can help you.'

'Who are you? And how can you help me?'

'My name is Sherlock Holmes. And It's my **job** to know things other people don't know.'

'But, you can't know anything about this!'

'Excuse me, I know everything. You want to find twenty-four geese. Mrs Oakshott of Brixton Road sold them to Mr Breckinridge here. He sold them to Mr Windigate, the owner of the Alpha, and Mr Windigate sold them to the people in his goose club.'

'Oh, sir. This is wonderful. I'm very happy to meet you,' said the little man excitedly. 'You are right. I *am* very interested in those geese. More than I can say.'

'Why don't we go to a warm room in my house for a talk then? I don't like standing here in the cold street.'

Holmes put out his arm
and a **cab** stopped for us.

'But before we go, can you
please tell us your name?'

The little man looked at Holmes
and then at me before he answered.

'J-J-John Robinson,' he said.

'No, no,' said Holmes quietly. 'We'd like
to know your **real** name please.'

The stranger's face changed from white to red.

'Very well. My real name is James Ryder,' he said.

'Well, well, well,' said Holmes. 'Assistant Manager of the
Cosmopolitan Hotel. Now let's get into the cab and go
home. Then I can tell you everything you want to know.'

So we got into the cab and went home. Ryder looked excited
but said nothing. Holmes didn't speak at all in the cab.

cab a taxi

real not false

READING CHECK

Correct seven more mistakes in this summary of Chapter 5.

street

Holmes and Watson talk in the ~~hotel~~ near Breckinridge's shop. Holmes is happy to get Countess

Morcar's address. Behind them they hear Mr Breckinridge singing in front of his shop with a

big man. This man is very interested in Mrs Oakshott's dogs. Mr Breckinridge gets angry with

him. Holmes tells the man that he knows nothing about the case. The man says his name is

John Redman, but his real name is James Ryder. Holmes, Watson and Ryder go back to

Watson's house.

WORD WORK

Match the words in the magnifying glass with the underlined words in the sentences.

JOB

Weak

CABS

REAL

SHOUTED

a She was very <u>tired</u> after being ill. ...weak...

b He <u>spoke angrily</u> across the room at her. ....

c London <u>taxis</u> are usually black. ....

d What <u>work</u> does your father do, boy? ....

e Is this a <u>true</u> story? ....

GUESS WHAT

What happens in the next chapter? Tick the boxes.

a At home Holmes takes out . . .
- ☐ a letter from the Countess.
- ☐ the blue diamond.
- ☐ a gun.

b Ryder has . . . .
- ☐ a drink.
- ☐ a sandwich.
- ☐ a cigarette.

c We learn that . . . was the diamond thief.
- ☐ Ryder
- ☐ Horner
- ☐ Mrs Oakshott

d In the end . . . goes to prison.
- ☐ Ryder
- ☐ Horner
- ☐ no-one

CHAPTER 6 *One or two questions*

When we arrived at 221B Baker Street, we got out of the cab and went in. Back in his sitting room, Holmes spoke at last.

'Please sit down, Mr Ryder. Now, where were we? Ah, yes. You want to know what happened to those twenty-four geese. Or perhaps, what happened to one of those geese? You are interested in only one bird, I think. A white goose with a black **tail**.'

'Oh, sir,' Ryder said excitedly. 'Where did that bird go to?'

'It came here. And it was a most interesting bird. We found something in it after it died. The most wonderful thing. Here it is.'

tail the long thing at the back of an animal's body

Our visitor stood up weakly. Holmes opened his safe and took out the blue diamond. In his hand it was cold and beautiful. Ryder looked at the jewel but said nothing.

Holmes spoke for him. 'We know it was you, Ryder,' he said. 'Sit down and have a drink. You look very weak.'

I gave Ryder a drink. He sat down and drank it quickly and looked at Holmes. I saw he was afraid.

'You don't need to tell me much,' said Holmes, 'I know nearly everything about the case. But I have one or two questions to ask. How did you hear of the Countess of Morcar's blue diamond?'

'Catherine Cusack, her maid, told me,' said Ryder.

'I see,' Holmes went on. 'So you and Cusack wanted to get the diamond and sell it for lots of money. You asked John Horner to come and repair the window in the room because you knew of his time in prison. When he left, you took the diamond from the Countess's jewel box. Then you called the police. They came at once. Because of Horner's time in prison they believed he was the thief. It was all very easy. Then . . .'

'Oh, please, please!' cried Ryder, now on the **floor** at Holmes's feet. 'Think of my father! Think of my mother! I never did anything wrong before. I'm never going to do it again. Please don't tell the police. I don't want to go to prison.'

'Sit down in your chair!' said Holmes coldly. 'You're crying now, but did you **feel sorry for** young Horner? He knew nothing of this crime. But the police believed he was a diamond thief, and so he went to court and he is now going to prison – all because of you.'

'I can leave the country, Mr Holmes. Then, when I don't go to court, Horner can leave prison.'

floor the place in a room where you stand and walk

feel sorry for to be unhappy about

'We can see about that later!' said Holmes. 'But now please tell me, Mr Ryder. How did the diamond get from the hotel into a goose? And how did the goose get into a shop? And please tell the **truth**.'

Ryder began:

When the police **arrested** Horner, I left the hotel with the diamond in my pocket. I didn't want to stay at the Cosmopolitan, not with the police everywhere, looking at everything, so I went to my sister's house in South London. She lives in Brixton Road with her husband, Mr Oakshott. I saw lots of **police officers** on my way there and when I got to Brixton Road I was very afraid.

'What's the matter?' my sister asked.

I told her about the diamond thief and about the police arresting Horner. Then I went into the back garden to smoke and think. What could I do with the diamond now? In the garden, I remembered my friend Maudsley. He began well, but he went bad, and in the end he went to prison for his crimes. 'Perhaps he knows about selling diamonds,' I thought. So I **decided** to visit him at his home in Kilburn in North London.

'But how can I walk across London with the diamond?' I thought. 'I can't have it in my pocket. Not with all those police officers in the streets.' Then I looked down at the geese in the garden and I thought of something.

I knew one of those geese was for me, for my Christmas dinner. So I decided to take my goose there and then, and not to wait for it.

I quickly **caught** a big white goose with a black tail. Then I took the diamond from my pocket, and put it into the bird's mouth. I felt the jewel go down its **neck**. With

truth when what you say is true

arrest to take a person to prison

police officers policemen and policewomen

decide to think about something and then do it

catch (*past* **caught**) to take quickly in your hands

neck this is between your head and your body

the   diamond
now inside the
goose I felt happy. I could
walk to Kilburn and
back easily.

Then my sister came into the garden.

'What are you doing with that goose?' she said.

I put my bird down and it ran off with the other
geese. 'That's the goose I want for Christmas,' I said.

'Very well. Catch it, kill it, and take it with you,'
she said.

Well, Mr Holmes. I caught that bird, killed it and
took it with me to Kilburn. There I told my friend Maudsley
all about the diamond and he laughed and laughed. We got
a knife and opened the goose but we couldn't find the
diamond. I knew then something was wrong.

I left the goose with Maudsley, ran to my sister's house, and went into the back garden. There were no geese there.

'Where are they all, Maggie?' I said.

'In Mr Breckinridge's shop, in Covent Garden.'

'Were there two birds with black tails?' I asked.

'Yes, there were, James,' she said. 'And to my eyes one was no different from the other.'

I understood it all then. The diamond was inside the other goose with the black tail. And that goose was now in Mr Breckinridge's shop. I ran to Covent Garden at once and went to Breckinridge's. But the geese weren't in his shop, and when I asked about them he told me: 'I sold them all at once.'

'But you must tell me. Where are they now?' I asked again and again. But he never told me. You and Dr Watson heard him earlier tonight, Mr Holmes. He never answered my questions.

'Now my sister thinks I'm a terrible brother. I'm a thief, I'm going to lose my good name, and I never got any money from my crime at all. Oh, what's going to happen to me?'

He put his head in his hands and began to cry.

Holmes didn't speak for a long time. Then, in the end, he stood up and opened the door.

'Get out!' he said.

'Oh, thank you! Thank you, sir!' said Ryder.

'Be quiet and get out!' said Holmes again, and, with that, Ryder ran out of the door, downstairs, out into the street, and away.

'After all, Watson,' said Holmes. 'It's not my job to do the police's work for them and young Horner's going to be all right. Ryder isn't going to go to court now.

Without him, the police have no **witness** to say Horner was the thief.

'Perhaps I'm doing something wrong, but I don't believe it. I think I'm helping Ryder to be a better man. Send him to prison now and you make him into a thief for life. But now he's afraid, he's not going to go wrong again. We found the **solution** to the crime and that makes me happy. And it's Christmas, after all, and Christmas is a time to be nice to other people, I believe.

'And now, Watson, let's ask Mrs Hudson to bring in our dinner.'

witness a person who saw a crime

solution the answer to a problem

READING CHECK

What do they say?
Complete the sentences.

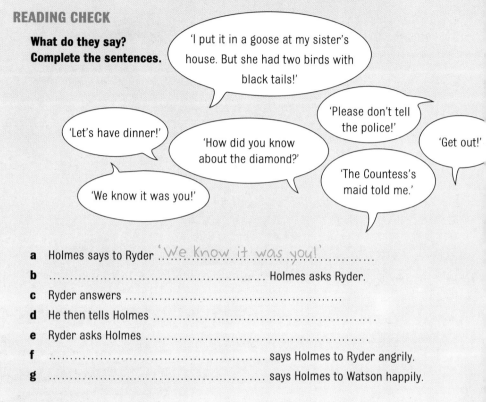

'I put it in a goose at my sister's house. But she had two birds with black tails!'

'Please don't tell the police!'

'Let's have dinner!'

'How did you know about the diamond?'

'Get out!'

'The Countess's maid told me.'

'We know it was you!'

a Holmes says to Ryder 'We know it was you!'

b .... Holmes asks Ryder.

c Ryder answers ....

d He then tells Holmes ....

e Ryder asks Holmes ....

f .... says Holmes to Ryder angrily.

g .... says Holmes to Watson happily.

WORD WORK

Find words to complete the sentences on page 39.

0	D	B	D	P	J	U	T	G	S	V	Z	U	Y
F	E	E	L	S	O	R	R	Y	F	O	R	O	T
K	C	G	E	S	I	E	U	S	C	V	E	M	F
S	I	G	E	R	W	I	T	N	E	S	S	E	S
A	D	O	T	S	H	O	H	U	I	N	E	C	K
K	E	F	A	H	D	X	N	S	I	J	C	L	E
P	O	L	I	C	E	O	F	F	I	C	E	R	S
Z	W	O	L	A	Q	U	O	G	D	A	H	Y	C
L	U	O	V	B	E	S	O	L	U	T	I	O	N
A	R	R	E	S	T	L	U	R	Y	C	F	E	J
H	O	J	L	E	W	X	I	Z	P	H	U	W	S

a Why does Holmes _decide_ to help Ryder?

b Does he _ _ _ _ _ _ _ _ _ _ _ _ _ that young and unhappy man?

c In the end it's always good to tell the _ _ _ _ _ _ .

d I think _ _ _ _ _ _ _ _ _ _ _ _ _ _ _ _ don't have an easy job.

e A good detective finds the _ _ _ _ _ _ _ _ to every case.

f Ryder doesn't _ _ _ _ _ _ the right goose.

g Henry Baker's goose was white with a black _ _ _ _ too.

h The police don't _ _ _ _ _ _ _ Ryder because he leaves England.

i With no _ _ _ _ _ _ _ _ _ _ to speak in Court, the police can't put Horner in prison.

j Ryder gets on the _ _ _ _ _ _ at Holmes's feet.

k Ryder puts the diamond down the goose's _ _ _ _ _ .

GUESS WHAT

1 **Here are some other Sherlock Holmes cases. What are they about? Match the sentences with the titles.**

a . . . Sherlock Holmes dies in Switzerland . . . or does he?

b . . . four men from India come to England to find the jewels they lost years ago . . .

c . . . someone moves into the old house opposite 221B but he doesn't want people to know he is there . . .

d . . . things begin when a rich man and his wife find little pictures of people on the walls of their house . . .

2 **Which of these books would you like to read?**

PROJECT A

My favourite detective

1 **Here are some detectives from books, films and on TV. Who do you like best? Why?**

Jessica Fletcher

Hercule Poirot

Fox Mulder and
Dana Scully

Inspector Gadget

2 **Read the poster about Sherlock Holmes on page 41 and complete the table.**

Name:	Sherlock Holmes	
Home:		
Appearance:		
Usual Clothes:		
Habits:		
Hobbies:		

3 **Complete the table about your detective.**

Sherlock Holmes . . .

. . . lives in Baker Street in London with his housekeeper, Mrs Hudson.

. . . is tall and thin.

. . . plays music in his free time.

. . . can look very different when he wants.

. . . wears a hat and coat when it's cold.

. . . smokes.

4   **Make a poster about your favourite detective.**

PROJECT B

A CRIME REPORT

1 Read the report.

MONA LISA DISAPPEARS!

In 1911 someone took the famous picture 'Mona Lisa' by Leonardo da Vinci from the Louvre museum in Paris.

The police arrested and questioned the writer Guillaume Apollinaire but he was innocent of the crime.

Later the police found the real thief when he tried to sell the picture in Florence, Italy in 1913. He was a poor Italian. His name was Vincenzo Perugia.